M000072782

Inspired by the major motion picture

LETTERS TO GOD

Journal

ZONDERVAN

Letters to God Journal
Copyright © 2010 by Possibility Pictures, LLC

Requests for information should be addressed to:
Zondervan, *Grand Rapids, Michigan* 49530

ISBN 978-0-310-72002-7

Introduction: Lyn Cryderman
Cover design: Extra Credit Projects
Interior design: Carlos Eluterio Estrada

Printed in China

10 11 12 13 14 15 /GPC/ 6 5 4 3 2 1

Prayer: Your Letter to God

In the movie *Letters to God*, nine-year-old Tyler Doherty came up with an unusual way to pray for his friends and family—he wrote each prayer as a letter, put it in an envelope addressed simply to "God," and then stuffed it in the mailbox where it eventually ended up in a dead letter bin at the post office. Except at this particular post office, the manager retrieved the letters and handed them to an inexperienced mailman with a drinking problem and jaded outlook on life. As the movie progresses, Tyler prays for his new mailman to get his life back on track, while Tyler's family and friends pray for Tyler to be healed of cancer. One prayer gets answered while another appears to be ignored.

Few things in our lives are as simple and complex as the subject of prayer. What is it? How does it work? *Does* it work? Whose prayers get answered and why? Tyler's explanation of why he wrote his prayers to God is a good place to begin: "It's my favorite way to talk to God. It's like texting your best friend."

Why we pray

Prayer is one of those things we do even if we don't quite understand it. Whenever there is a personal or national tragedy, even people who don't care much for religion seem to pray. A high school student clings for life in a hospital room following a terrible automobile accident, and his friends spread the word: "Say a prayer for Ryan." At the end of her report on a tsunami that killed hundreds of people, the anchorwoman says, "Our prayers are with the victims' families."

Prayer often seems like the right thing to do, and people from all walks of life appear to be comfortable doing it. Mothers and fathers pray for their children as they send them off to school. Teenagers pray for courage to live out their faith. There's a good chance your neighbor prays, as does your best friend, your doctor, or your teacher. Every president in our lifetime has acknowledged praying for wisdom.

We pray with varying degrees of hope that someone might be listening.

The Bible reassures us that someone, indeed, is listening: God. Just before Moses was given the Ten Commandments, he gathered his followers together to teach them about God, saying to them, "What other nation is so great as to have their gods near them the way the LORD our God is near us whenever we pray to him?" (Deuteronomy 4:7). In a time in history when people worshiped many different gods who were distant and unresponsive, Moses reminded his people (and us) that the one true God is always close when we pray to him. Let that sink in for a moment: the Lord our God is near you whenever you pray to him.

We also pray, because it strengthens our relationship with God. In this day of instant communication through cell phones and email, could you imagine not staying in touch with a close friend? When we accept God's gift of salvation, we enter into a personal relationship with him, and, like any relationship, it grows stronger through conversation. As Christians, we have the blessed hope of one day joining God in heaven. Until then, we can rely on prayer to stay close to him. Since God is always present, we can pray to him anywhere and anytime and know that he is right there with us. Prayer is our lifeline to God.

Christians pray because God invites us to. He cares about us as individuals, and about every detail in our lives. The Psalmist encourages you to "Cast your cares on the Lord and he will sustain you" (Psalm 55:22). This wonderful, mysterious thing called prayer was God's idea. It's not an obligation or a ritual we have to perform, but a gift to us so that we may have fellowship with him and never have to face anything alone. Even in the face of hardship and death, we can say as King David said, "you are with me."

Most of us know the importance of prayer, yet we often struggle to make it a part of our daily lives. Prayer for many of us is like exercise—we know we should do it regularly because it's good for us, but more often than not, we decide to skip it, promising ourselves we'll do it tomorrow. When we become sporadic in our efforts to exercise regularly, we might look for ways to revitalize our routine, like trying a new way to work out. Instead of jogging, we switch to bicycling, and it gets us back in the habit of exercising.

Just like exercising routines, there are many different ways to pray—sometimes all you need is a new approach.

Writing your letters to God

Revitalize your prayer life by writing your prayers out as letters to God. When Tyler wrote his prayers as letters, he was continuing a tradition that goes back to the Book of Psalms, where the writer—which many people believe to be King David—penned his questions, complaints, and praises to God.

This journal gives you the opportunity to do the same thing. Have you ever found that when you pray out loud or in your head, your mind wanders off or you get distracted and seem to just be repeating words without really thinking about it? *The physical act of putting pen to paper can focus your mind on what you want to say and keep your attention on God.*

Writing your prayers can also add some variety to your regular time with God. As you use this journal, consider alternating between writing your prayers one day and praying as you normally would the next. You may even discover types of prayer that felt intimidating in the traditional way feel more comfortable when written out.

Finally, writing your prayers in this journal gives you a permanent record of your relationship with God —a spiritual diary of your conversations. By the time you get to the last page of this journal, you will have written your own "Book of Psalms" to God. *Writing your own letters to God allows you to look back on your prayer life and see how God responded to you.*

Does writing your prayers make them more effective or guarantee the best answer? Not at all; God listens to all of our prayers—written or spoken—and answers according to his will. Think about taking time before each writing session to read some of your previous prayers, and, if you have received an answer, make a note of it on the page. You may find that by looking over your prayers in this way, God's provision and care will surprise you.

Getting started

As you begin, remember that you are writing a letter, not an assignment for your English teacher. No one is going to go over your prayers with a red pen or give you a grade. **Relax and write from your heart.** Don't try to impress God by writing in flowery language because you feel that's what God expects. In fact, Jesus warned against trying to impress people with your prayers. If you were writing a letter to your best friend, you would want to sound like the person you really are, and you would share things that are important to you. God wants the same kind of relationship. Tell God what's going on in your life and what you would like him to do for you.

Consider one of Tyler's prayers from the movie:

Dear God, I feel yucky today but Sam wants to climb trees. I already threw up three times this morning though. Sam's going to need another friend, you know. Her grandfather is a lot of fun, but I don't think he can climb trees.

Your prayers don't have to be profound or deal with weighty topics. God wants to walk in your shoes with you; to help you deal with what's important to you. Before you begin to write, spend some time in silence and then make a list of things that you want to talk to God about. Imagine what you would say if God was right there beside you and asked, "How can I help you today?"

It's also a good idea to find a quiet, comfortable place to write your letters to God so that you won't be distracted. In his Sermon on the Mount, Jesus taught that "... when you pray, go into your room, close the door and pray to your Father" (Matthew 6:6). Some of the great prayer warriors of previous centuries actually went into their closets to pray. Think about what works best for you: If you're a morning person, where do you like to sit and gather your thoughts before the day begins? If you're a night person, where's that corner in your house or apartment where you can unwind and reflect on your day? Do you enjoy hanging out at a coffee shop to relax with a good book? All of these places would be perfect for writing your letters to God.

If you are not sure what to write in your letters, consider using the popular acronym A-C-T-S as a template for your prayers: **A**doration (praising God for all that he means to us), **C**onfession (telling him the things we have done wrong and for which we are sorry), **T**hanksgiving (reminding him of the things we are thankful for), and **S**upplication (asking him to meet a need we or someone else has). If things are happening in your life that seem unfair, or if you feel that God is distant and unresponsive, tell him. If you are angry at God because you think he allowed something bad to happen to you or a loved one, don't hold back. Too many people think that prayer has to be safe—that we can't unload our real burdens on God. They obviously haven't read the Psalms:

"Why, O LORD, do you stand far off? Why do you hide yourself in times of trouble?" (Psalm 10:1)

"How long, O LORD? Will you forget me forever?" (Psalm 13:1)

"My God, my God, why have you forsaken me? Why are you so far from saving me, so far from the words of my groaning? O my God, I cry out by day, but you do not answer ..." (Psalm 22:1–2)

You may feel the same way King David did and write it this way in your letter to God:

How come you seem so far away whenever I talk to you? Are you ever going to answer me?

Hey, God! Remember me? It sure would be nice if you could find the time to answer me.

God. GOD! I'm really hurting, but you don't seem to care. What's going on?

When you write a letter to a friend, you can hardly wait to get an answer, and the same is true of prayer. We want to hear back from God, but sometimes we forget to check the mailbox: we say a prayer and then quickly go back to what we were doing.

When you write your letters to God, spend some time in silence listening for his answer. And as you go through your day, continue listening by looking for his answers, which may come to you in unexpected ways. There may be times when God shouts to us in a voice we can clearly hear, but most of the time he chooses to whisper in a "still, small, voice," and if we don't pay attention, we might miss it.

For instance, God's gentle whisper might actually be the voice of a trusted spiritual mentor or Christian friend whose advice becomes the answer to your prayer. Unless you write about something deeply personal or private, consider letting someone close to you read your letters to God. Not only can they join you in praying for needs in your life, but they may be able to help you hear God's answers.

God also sometimes whispers his answers as thoughts that seem to appear in our minds for no reason. For example, you might ask God to help you resolve a conflict you've had with someone and all you can think about for the next few days is buying a funny greeting card and sending it to that person. Did that thought just come out of the blue? Perhaps. But if you feel led to take a particular course of action, it doesn't conflict with God's righteousness or character, and you just can't seem to get it out of your mind, you are likely hearing from God. This is why it is especially important to always spend some time listening to God after you pray to him. As Thomas Merton wrote, "Silence is the first language of God." If you just write your letters to God and then head off into your busy day, it will be difficult to hear his answer.

Finally, God also speaks to us by opening and closing doors of opportunity. Many people pray, "God, if you want me to do that, you will have to provide the way." If you pray like that and a door is opened for you, step through it and continue walking until he closes the next door. When God closes a door for us, it is his way of saying, "Not yet," or, "I have something better for you."

God promises to listen to and answer our prayers, and we can trust him to keep his word because he is "faithful to all his promises and loving toward all he has made" (Psalm 145:13). His answer may not be the one we wanted or expected, but it will be the best—one that allows you to be part of his grand redemptive plan for the world.

The beautiful thing about prayer is that nothing is off limits. ***God welcomes your questions and complaints as much as he loves hearing your praise and thanksgiving.*** He desires to meet you in your time of need and comfort you when you call out to him. From the simple story of a little boy who addressed his letters to "God," we are reminded that it's not only our words that matter, but our faith that sends them straight to the heart of our Lord in heaven.

_____

_____

_____

_____

_____

_____

_____

_____

_____

_____

_____

_____

_____

_____

_____

_____

_____

_____

_____

_____

_____

_____

God speaks in the silence of the heart. Listening is the beginning of prayer.

Mother Teresa

_____

_____

_____

_____

_____

_____

_____

_____

_____

_____

_____

_____

_____

_____

_____

_____

_____

_____

_____

_____

_____

_____

_____

_____

Let us then approach the throne of grace with confidence, so that we may receive mercy and find grace to help us in our time of need.

Hebrews 4:16

_____

_____

_____

_____

_____

_____

_____

_____

_____

_____

_____

_____

_____

_____

_____

_____

_____

_____

_____

_____

_____

_____

_____

Do not be anxious about anything, but in everything, by prayer and petition, with thanksgiving, present your requests to God. And the peace of God, which transcends all understanding, will guard your hearts and your minds in Christ Jesus.

Philippians 4:6–7

_____

_____

_____

_____

_____

_____

_____

_____

_____

_____

_____

_____

_____

_____

_____

_____

_____

_____

_____

_____

_____

_____

[Jesus] is strong ... but He's also approachable. He is able to carry our load ... but He'll never make us feel embarrassed or defeated for asking.

Joni Eareckson Tada

_____

_____

_____

_____

_____

_____

_____

_____

_____

_____

_____

_____

_____

_____

_____

_____

_____

_____

_____

_____

_____

_____

_____

_____

You are the God who performs miracles; you display your power among the peoples.

Psalm 77:14

_____

_____

_____

_____

_____

_____

_____

_____

_____

_____

_____

_____

_____

_____

_____

_____

_____

_____

_____

_____

_____

_____

This is the confidence we have in approaching God: that if we ask anything according to his will, he hears us. And if we know that he hears us—whatever we ask—we know that we have what we asked of him.

1 John 5:14–15

_____

_____

_____

_____

_____

_____

_____

_____

_____

_____

_____

_____

_____

_____

_____

_____

_____

_____

_____

_____

_____

_____

In place of our exhaustion and spiritual fatigue, God will give us rest. All he asks is that we come to him ... that we spend a while thinking about him, meditating on him, talking to him, listening in silence.

Charles Swindoll

Be joyful always; pray continually; give thanks in all circumstances, for this is God's will for you in Christ Jesus.

1 Thessalonians 5:16–18

_____

_____

_____

_____

_____

_____

_____

_____

_____

_____

_____

_____

_____

_____

_____

_____

_____

_____

_____

_____

_____

_____

_____

The LORD has heard my cry for mercy; the LORD accepts my prayer.

Psalm 6:9

_____

_____

_____

_____

_____

_____

_____

_____

_____

_____

_____

_____

_____

_____

_____

_____

_____

_____

_____

_____

_____

_____

Begin the day with the Word of God and prayer, and get first of all into harmony with Him.

James Hudson Taylor

_____

_____

_____

_____

_____

_____

_____

_____

_____

_____

_____

_____

_____

_____

_____

_____

_____

_____

_____

_____

_____

_____

_____

But I call to God, and the LORD saves me. Evening, morning and noon I cry out in distress, and he hears my voice.

Psalm 55:16–17

_____

_____

_____

_____

_____

_____

_____

_____

_____

_____

_____

_____

_____

_____

_____

_____

_____

_____

_____

_____

_____

_____

Then you will call upon me and come and pray to me, and I will listen to you.

Jeremiah 29:12

_____

_____

_____

_____

_____

_____

_____

_____

_____

_____

_____

_____

_____

_____

_____

_____

_____

_____

_____

_____

_____

_____

_____

_____

Prayer allows me to admit my failures, weaknesses, and limitations to One who responds to human vulnerability with infinite mercy.

Philip Yancey

_____

_____

_____

_____

_____

_____

_____

_____

_____

_____

_____

_____

_____

_____

_____

_____

_____

_____

_____

_____

In the same way, the Spirit helps us in our weakness. We do not know what we ought to pray for, but the Spirit himself intercedes for us with groans that words cannot express.

Romans 8:26

Devote yourselves to prayer, being watchful and thankful.

Colossians 4:2

_____

_____

_____

_____

_____

_____

_____

_____

_____

_____

_____

_____

_____

_____

_____

_____

_____

_____

_____

_____

_____

_____

_____

Avail yourself of the greatest privilege this side of heaven. Jesus Christ died to make this communion and communication with the Father possible.

Billy Graham

_____

_____

_____

_____

_____

_____

_____

_____

_____

_____

_____

_____

_____

_____

_____

_____

_____

_____

_____

_____

_____

_____

_____

_____

God speaks in the silence of the heart. Listening is the beginning of prayer.

Mother Teres

_____

_____

_____

_____

_____

_____

_____

_____

_____

_____

_____

_____

_____

_____

_____

_____

_____

_____

_____

_____

_____

_____

Let us then approach the throne of grace with confidence, so that we may receive mercy and find grace to help us in our time of need.

Hebrews 4:16

_____

_____

_____

_____

_____

_____

_____

_____

_____

_____

_____

_____

_____

_____

_____

_____

_____

_____

_____

_____

_____

_____

Do not be anxious about anything, but in everything, by prayer and petition, with thanksgiving, present your requests to God. And the peace of God, which transcends all understanding, will guard your hearts and your minds in Christ Jesus.

Philippians 4:6–7

_____

_____

_____

_____

_____

_____

_____

_____

_____

_____

_____

_____

_____

_____

_____

_____

_____

_____

_____

_____

_____

_____

_____

[Jesus] is strong ... but He's also approachable. He is able to carry our load ... but He'll never make us feel embarrassed or defeated for asking.

Joni Eareckson Tada

_____

_____

_____

_____

_____

_____

_____

_____

_____

_____

_____

_____

_____

_____

_____

_____

_____

_____

_____

_____

_____

_____

_____

You are the God who performs miracles; you display your power among the peoples.

Psalm 77:14

_____

_____

_____

_____

_____

_____

_____

_____

_____

_____

_____

_____

_____

_____

_____

_____

_____

_____

_____

_____

_____

_____

_____

This is the confidence we have in approaching God: that if we ask anything according to his will, he hears us. And if we know that he hears us—whatever we ask—we know that we have what we asked of him.

1 John 5:14–15

_____

_____

_____

_____

_____

_____

_____

_____

_____

_____

_____

_____

_____

_____

_____

_____

_____

_____

_____

_____

_____

In place of our exhaustion and spiritual fatigue, God will give us rest. All he asks is that we come to him … that we spend a while thinking about him, meditating on him, talking to him, listening in silence.

Charles Swindoll

_____
_____
_____
_____
_____
_____
_____
_____
_____
_____
_____
_____
_____
_____
_____
_____
_____
_____
_____
_____
_____
_____

Be joyful always; pray continually; give thanks in all circumstances, for this is God's will for you in Christ Jesus.

1 Thessalonians 5:16–18

_____

_____

_____

_____

_____

_____

_____

_____

_____

_____

_____

_____

_____

_____

_____

_____

_____

_____

_____

_____

_____

_____

_____

The LORD has heard my cry for mercy; the LORD accepts my prayer.

Psalm 6:9

_____

_____

_____

_____

_____

_____

_____

_____

_____

_____

_____

_____

_____

_____

_____

_____

_____

_____

_____

_____

_____

_____

Begin the day with the Word of God and prayer, and get first of all into harmony with Him.

James Hudson Taylor

_____

_____

_____

_____

_____

_____

_____

_____

_____

_____

_____

_____

_____

_____

_____

_____

_____

_____

_____

_____

_____

_____

_____

But I call to God, and the LORD saves me. Evening, morning and noon I cry out in distress, and he hears my voice.

Psalm 55:16–17

_____

_____

_____

_____

_____

_____

_____

_____

_____

_____

_____

_____

_____

_____

_____

_____

_____

_____

_____

_____

_____

_____

Then you will call upon me and come and pray to me, and I will listen to you.

Jeremiah 29:12

_____

_____

_____

_____

_____

_____

_____

_____

_____

_____

_____

_____

_____

_____

_____

_____

_____

_____

_____

_____

_____

_____

Prayer allows me to admit my failures, weaknesses, and limitations to One who responds to human vulnerability with infinite mercy.

Philip Yancey

_____

_____

_____

_____

_____

_____

_____

_____

_____

_____

_____

_____

_____

_____

_____

_____

_____

_____

_____

_____

_____

_____

_____

In the same way, the Spirit helps us in our weakness. We do not know what we ought to pray for, but the Spirit himself intercedes for us with groans that words cannot express.

Romans 8:26

_____

_____

_____

_____

_____

_____

_____

_____

_____

_____

_____

_____

_____

_____

_____

_____

_____

_____

_____

_____

_____

_____

_____

_____

Devote yourselves to prayer, being watchful and thankful.

Colossians 4:2

_____

_____

_____

_____

_____

_____

_____

_____

_____

_____

_____

_____

_____

_____

_____

_____

_____

_____

_____

_____

_____

_____

_____

_____

Avail yourself of the greatest privilege this side of heaven. Jesus Christ died to make this communion and communication with the Father possible.

Billy Graham

God speaks in the silence of the heart. Listening is the beginning of prayer.

Mother Teresa

_____

_____

_____

_____

_____

_____

_____

_____

_____

_____

_____

_____

_____

_____

_____

_____

_____

_____

_____

_____

_____

_____

_____

_____

_____

Let us then approach the throne of grace with confidence, so that we may receive mercy and find grace to help us in our time of need.

Hebrews 4:16

_____

_____

_____

_____

_____

_____

_____

_____

_____

_____

_____

_____

_____

_____

_____

_____

_____

_____

_____

_____

_____

_____

_____

Do not be anxious about anything, but in everything, by prayer and petition, with thanksgiving, present your requests to God. And the peace of God, which transcends all understanding, will guard your hearts and your minds in Christ Jesus.

Philippians 4:6–7

_____

_____

_____

_____

_____

_____

_____

_____

_____

_____

_____

_____

_____

_____

_____

_____

_____

_____

_____

_____

_____

_____

_____

_____

[Jesus] is strong ... but He's also approachable. He is able to carry our load ... but He'll never make us feel embarrassed or defeated for asking.

Joni Eareckson Tada

_____

_____

_____

_____

_____

_____

_____

_____

_____

_____

_____

_____

_____

_____

_____

_____

_____

_____

_____

_____

_____

_____

_____

_____

You are the God who performs miracles; you display your power among the peoples.

Psalm 77:14

_____

_____

_____

_____

_____

_____

_____

_____

_____

_____

_____

_____

_____

_____

_____

_____

_____

_____

_____

_____

_____

_____

_____

This is the confidence we have in approaching God: that if we ask anything according to his will, he hears us. And if we know that he hears us—whatever we ask—we know that we have what we asked of him.

1 John 5:14–15

_____

_____

_____

_____

_____

_____

_____

_____

_____

_____

_____

_____

_____

_____

_____

_____

_____

_____

_____

_____

_____

_____

_____

In place of our exhaustion and spiritual fatigue, God will give us rest. All he asks is that we come to him ... that we spend a while thinking about him, meditating on him, talking to him, listening in silence.

Charles Swindoll

_____

_____

_____

_____

_____

_____

_____

_____

_____

_____

_____

_____

_____

_____

_____

_____

_____

_____

_____

_____

_____

_____

Be joyful always; pray continually; give thanks in all circumstances, for this is God's will for you in Christ Jesus.

1 Thessalonians 5:16–18

_____

_____

_____

_____

_____

_____

_____

_____

_____

_____

_____

_____

_____

_____

_____

_____

_____

_____

_____

_____

_____

_____

_____

_____

_____

The LORD has heard my cry for mercy; the LORD accepts my prayer.

Psalm 6:9

_____

_____

_____

_____

_____

_____

_____

_____

_____

_____

_____

_____

_____

_____

_____

_____

_____

_____

_____

_____

_____

_____

Begin the day with the Word of God and prayer, and get first of all into harmony with Him.

James Hudson Taylor

_____

_____

_____

_____

_____

_____

_____

_____

_____

_____

_____

_____

_____

_____

_____

_____

_____

_____

_____

_____

_____

_____

_____

But I call to God, and the LORD saves me. Evening, morning and noon I cry out in distress, and he hears my voice.

Psalm 55:16–17

_____

_____

_____

_____

_____

_____

_____

_____

_____

_____

_____

_____

_____

_____

_____

_____

_____

_____

_____

_____

_____

_____

_____

_____

Then you will call upon me and come and pray to me, and I will listen to you.

Jeremiah 29:12

_____

_____

_____

_____

_____

_____

_____

_____

_____

_____

_____

_____

_____

_____

_____

_____

_____

_____

_____

_____

_____

_____

Prayer allows me to admit my failures, weaknesses, and limitations to One who responds to human vulnerability with infinite mercy.

Philip Yancey

_____

_____

_____

_____

_____

_____

_____

_____

_____

_____

_____

_____

_____

_____

_____

_____

_____

_____

_____

_____

_____

_____

_____

_____

In the same way, the Spirit helps us in our weakness. We do not know what we ought to pray for, but the Spirit himself intercedes for us with groans that words cannot express.

Romans 8:26

_____

_____

_____

_____

_____

_____

_____

_____

_____

_____

_____

_____

_____

_____

_____

_____

_____

_____

_____

_____

_____

_____

Devote yourselves to prayer, being watchful and thankful.

Colossians 4:2

Avail yourself of the greatest privilege this side of heaven. Jesus Christ died to make this communion and communication with the Father possible.

Billy Graham

_____

_____

_____

_____

_____

_____

_____

_____

_____

_____

_____

_____

_____

_____

_____

_____

_____

_____

_____

_____

_____

_____

_____

God speaks in the silence of the heart. Listening is the beginning of prayer.

Mother Teresa

_____

_____

_____

_____

_____

_____

_____

_____

_____

_____

_____

_____

_____

_____

_____

_____

_____

_____

_____

_____

_____

_____

Let us then approach the throne of grace with confidence, so that we may receive mercy and find grace to help us in our time of need.

Hebrews 4:16

_____

_____

_____

_____

_____

_____

_____

_____

_____

_____

_____

_____

_____

_____

_____

_____

_____

_____

_____

_____

_____

_____

_____

Do not be anxious about anything, but in everything, by prayer and petition, with thanksgiving, present your requests to God. And the peace of God, which transcends all understanding, will guard your hearts and your minds in Christ Jesus.

Philippians 4:6–7

_____

_____

_____

_____

_____

_____

_____

_____

_____

_____

_____

_____

_____

_____

_____

_____

_____

_____

_____

_____

_____

_____

[Jesus] is strong ... but He's also approachable. He is able to carry our load ... but He'll never make us feel embarrassed or defeated for asking.

Joni Eareckson Tad.

_____

_____

_____

_____

_____

_____

_____

_____

_____

_____

_____

_____

_____

_____

_____

_____

_____

_____

_____

_____

_____

_____

_____

_____

    You are the God who performs miracles; you display your
power among the peoples.

Psalm 77:14

_____

_____

_____

_____

_____

_____

_____

_____

_____

_____

_____

_____

_____

_____

_____

_____

_____

_____

_____

_____

_____

This is the confidence we have in approaching God: that if we ask anything according to his will, he hears us. And if we know that he hears us—whatever we ask—we know that we have what we asked of him.

1 John 5:14–15

_____

_____

_____

_____

_____

_____

_____

_____

_____

_____

_____

_____

_____

_____

_____

_____

_____

_____

_____

_____

In place of our exhaustion and spiritual fatigue, God will give us rest. All he asks is that we come to him ... that we spend a while thinking about him, meditating on him, talking to him, listening in silence.

Charles Swindoll

_____

_____

_____

_____

_____

_____

_____

_____

_____

_____

_____

_____

_____

_____

_____

_____

_____

_____

_____

_____

_____

_____

_____

Be joyful always; pray continually; give thanks in all circumstances, for this is God's will for you in Christ Jesus.

1 Thessalonians 5:16–18

_____

_____

_____

_____

_____

_____

_____

_____

_____

_____

_____

_____

_____

_____

_____

_____

_____

_____

_____

_____

_____

_____

The LORD has heard my cry for mercy; the LORD accepts my prayer.

Psalm 6:9

_____

_____

_____

_____

_____

_____

_____

_____

_____

_____

_____

_____

_____

_____

_____

_____

_____

_____

_____

_____

_____

_____

Begin the day with the Word of God and prayer, and get first of all into harmony with Him.

James Hudson Taylor

_____

_____

_____

_____

_____

_____

_____

_____

_____

_____

_____

_____

_____

_____

_____

_____

_____

_____

_____

_____

_____

_____

_____

But I call to God, and the Lord saves me. Evening, morning and noon I cry out in distress, and he hears my voice.

Psalm 55:16–17

_____

_____

_____

_____

_____

_____

_____

_____

_____

_____

_____

_____

_____

_____

_____

_____

_____

_____

_____

_____

_____

_____

_____

_____

Then you will call upon me and come and pray to me, and I will listen to you.

Jeremiah 29:12

_____

_____

_____

_____

_____

_____

_____

_____

_____

_____

_____

_____

_____

_____

_____

_____

_____

_____

_____

_____

Prayer allows me to admit my failures, weaknesses, and limitations to One who responds to human vulnerability with infinite mercy.

Philip Yancey

_____

_____

_____

_____

_____

_____

_____

_____

_____

_____

_____

_____

_____

_____

_____

_____

_____

_____

_____

_____

_____

_____

_____

_____

In the same way, the Spirit helps us in our weakness. We do not know what we ought to pray for, but the Spirit himself intercedes for us with groans that words cannot express.

Romans 8:26

_____

_____

_____

_____

_____

_____

_____

_____

_____

_____

_____

_____

_____

_____

_____

_____

_____

_____

_____

_____

_____

_____

_____

Devote yourselves to prayer, being watchful and thankful.

Colossians 4:2

_____

_____

_____

_____

_____

_____

_____

_____

_____

_____

_____

_____

_____

_____

_____

_____

_____

_____

_____

_____

_____

_____

Avail yourself of the greatest privilege this side of heaven. Jesus Christ died to make this communion and communication with the Father possible.

Billy Graham

God speaks in the silence of the heart. Listening is the beginning of prayer.

Mother Teresa

_____

_____

_____

_____

_____

_____

_____

_____

_____

_____

_____

_____

_____

_____

_____

_____

_____

_____

_____

_____

_____

_____

_____

Let us then approach the throne of grace with confidence, so that we may receive mercy and find grace to help us in our time of need.

Hebrews 4:16

_____

_____

_____

_____

_____

_____

_____

_____

_____

_____

_____

_____

_____

_____

_____

_____

_____

_____

_____

_____

Do not be anxious about anything, but in everything, by prayer and petition, with thanksgiving, present your requests to God. And the peace of God, which transcends all understanding, will guard your hearts and your minds in Christ Jesus.

Philippians 4:6–7

_____

_____

_____

_____

_____

_____

_____

_____

_____

_____

_____

_____

_____

_____

_____

_____

_____

_____

_____

Avail yourself of the greatest privilege this side of heaven.
Jesus Christ died to make this communion and communication
with the Father possible.

Billy Graham